Au

STORIES FROM ANCIENT CIVILISATIONS

The Vikings

Published by Evans Brothers Limited
2A Portman Mansions
Chiltern Street
London W1U 6NR

© Evans Brothers Limited 2004
First published 2004
Printed in China

British Library Cataloguing in Publication Data

Husain, Shahrukh
    Stories from Ancient Civilisations: Vikings - (Stories
    from ancient civilisations)
    1. Mythology, Norse - Juvenile literature
    2. Civilization, Viking - Juvenile literature
    I. Title
    398.2'0948

ISBN 0 237 52446 5

CREDITS
Series Editor: Louise John
Editor: Julia Bird
Design: Robert Walster
Artworks: Bee Willey
Production: Jenny Mulvanny

STORIES FROM ANCIENT CIVILISATIONS

The Vikings

Shahrukh Husain
and Bee Willey

Evans

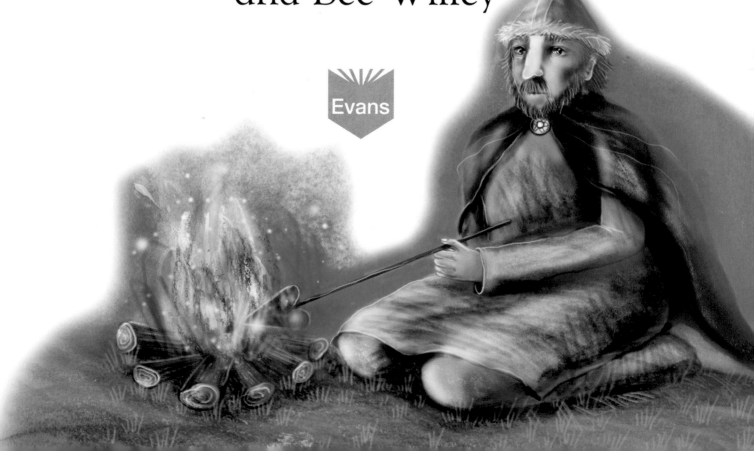

Introduction

Myths are probably the earliest stories ever told. People in ancient times used them to explain all that was important in life – how the universe was created, how the stars, sun, moon and planets appeared in the sky. To them these elements were gods whom they worshipped and whom they believed controlled their lives. They wanted to keep the gods happy to gain their blessings.

Myths are usually about important matters like birth, death and the afterlife and tend to have a moral. Viking warriors were fierce and daring in battle because death in battle was considered to be more honourable than death from sickness or old age. The Vikings believed that when heroes died fighting they went to Valhalla, the hall of heroes, ruled by the father of the gods, Odin. In Valhalla they feasted and revelled until Ragnarok, or the end of the world, when they would help the gods in a mighty clash between good and evil. The Viking Underworld, Hel, where people went after dying of sickness or old age, is described in the story of Baldur.

Like most people in ancient times, the Vikings travelled huge distances, searching for food and shelter. They voyaged over land and sea covering a vast part of the world, from Greenland in North America to Europe and the Middle East. When they conquered new lands, they usually brought their own gods and myths with them. As they settled, an exchange took place. They introduced their gods to the local people and in turn began to worship some of theirs. For example, Viking beliefs about dwarf craftsmen, magical blacksmiths and, most particularly, Odin, the father of the gods, can still be found in Britain today. In the Scandinavian homeland of the Vikings, the myths show a similar change of beliefs which is too old to trace. The ancient Vanir gods worshipped by the Vikings were replaced by the newer gods of the Aesir, but after a great war between the two races, described in many myths, the gods declared a truce and from then on mixed freely.

Viking myths are mostly about the adventures of the gods and how they fight the chaotic forces of nature, represented by frost giants, dragons and monsters. The myths also often describe encounters between the gods and humans, as for example Odin advises Prince Sigurd how to defeat the monster Fafnir.

Viking myths are part of the wider tradition of Norse mythology, which includes most of the Scandinavian countries, as well as other parts of Europe, particularly Germany. They are recorded in three collections, the anonymous Poetic Edda (late 13 CE), the Prose Edda, put together by Snorri Sturluson (early 13 CE) and in the verse of court poets known as skalds (900 CE - 1400 CE).

Contents

The Mother of Water

This account of the creation of the world is taken from the Finnish epic, Kalevala. Its fifty poems, which were written by Elias Lonrott in 1835, contain some of the oldest tales of Scandinavia.

BEFORE TIME BEGAN, A TEAL FLEW THROUGH SPACE, LOOKING FOR SOMEWHERE TO BUILD A NEST. She looked north and south, east and west but all she saw around her was churning water.

'If I lay my eggs on the waves, they'll drift away and smash,' she thought. 'If I lay them in the air, they'll be blown away. What shall I do?'

Deep down in the ocean, the Mother of Water heard her plea and raised her mighty knee above the water.

The teal saw the knee, lush with grass, high above the blue water. It was the perfect place for her nest. When it was built, she laid six eggs of gold and a seventh of iron. Then she perched on the eggs and began to brood.

On the first day, the eggs grew warm and the heat filtered through to the knee of the goddess. On the second day, her skin became hot. On the third, it began to scorch. In pain, she jerked her knee back under the sea. The eggs scattered from the nest, rolled into the water and smashed. Then slowly, as the teal and the goddess watched in amazement, they began to transform. The lower half of the eggs rose high above and formed the dome of the skies. The yolks gleamed and became the dazzling sun. The egg whites shimmered silver and formed the globe of the moon. The pieces of shell were transformed into a million stars and the iron scraps turned into dark clouds. And that was how the world was formed.

The Vikings called the sun goddess Sol and the moon god Mani. The two gods rode across the sky on horse-drawn chariots, chased by wolves, exchanging places at dawn and dusk. The Vikings believed that one day the wolves would catch the sun and the moon and swallow them, ending the cycle of night and day and bringing about the end of the world. The Vikings called the end of the world Ragnarok.

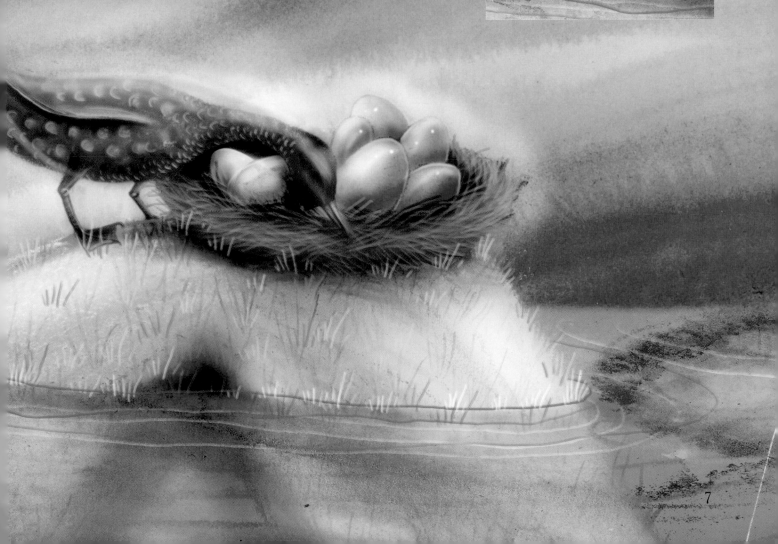

Ymir, the Frost Giant

The fight between the frost giants and the gods is another Viking tale of creation. It explains the bitter cold of Scandinavian countries and may even refer to one of the ice ages. The later Vikings travelled as far south as Turkey, so they knew that some lands were hot. The different climates in this story may reflect their experiences.

IN ANCIENT TIMES GINNUNGAGAP, THE GREAT VOID, DIVIDED FREEZING NIFLHEIM IN THE NORTH FROM BURNING MUSPELL IN THE SOUTH. One day, a river flowed into Niflheim from the warm south. At once, its waters froze. More and more water flowed into Niflheim until a strong floor of ice was formed between the two lands. Where hot and cold met, the ice thawed and formed a frost giant called Ymir.

Ymir stood up and stretched. From one enormous arm dropped a giant; from the other, a giantess. From his feet came a son. The ice, still melting, created a cow, Andhumla. The four hungry giants saw four rivers of milk flowing from her udders. They drank deeply until their bellies were full. Andhumla was hungry too, by now. She licked the icy rocks and tasted salt.

'I like this,' she thought. 'I'll have some more.' As she licked, she saw some hair. The next day she licked some more. A head came through the rocks. On the third day,

a body appeared. It was the god Buri. He soon had a son, Bor, who married a giantess. They had three sons called Odin, Vili and Ve.

'Ymir makes the world too cold,' complained Odin one day. 'Help me get rid of him.' His brothers agreed.

From Ymir's blood, Odin made rivers and oceans.

'Now help me put his body in the Great Void,' he told his brothers. There, Ymir's flesh became the earth and his bones the mountains. Odin lifted Ymir's skull high and created the sky. To light it, he caught the sparks that flew all the way to Niflheim from the fires of Muspell and they became the stars and planets. From Ymir's brains, Odin made dark storm-clouds.

Odin and his brothers looked proudly at their work. There was just one more job to be done. Odin took Ymir's eyebrows and built a large wall.

'This will keep the giants out,' he said.

The land within the wall was known as Midgard, or Middle Earth, where the human race would eventually come to live.

Odin and his family became the race of gods known as the Aesir. They lived in Asgard, Godland. One day as they walked along the seashore, they saw an ash tree and an elm tree and turned them into the first man and woman.

Odin and the Tree of Life

Odin, the father of the Viking gods, travelled the world helping people, disguised as an old man in a hood which hid his face. He carried a spear called Gungnir and wore a ring called Draupnir. Odin's pet ravens, Hugin and Munnin, brought him marvellous stories from their journeys but Odin was not satisfied. He wanted the power to know everything.

ODIN DECIDED TO VISIT MIMIR'S SPRING IN SEARCH OF GREATER WISDOM. He leapt astride eight-legged Sleipnir – the swiftest horse in the world – and together they flew across Bifrost, the rainbow bridge which linked Asgard to the famous tree Yggdrasil, at the centre of the world.

Odin jumped off his horse and strode towards the spring, which gushed beneath Yggdrasil. But every time he put his mouth to the bubbling water, it ceased to flow.

'What's the drink worth to you?' laughed the giant Mimir, who guarded the spring.

'Whatever it takes,' Odin vowed.

'Something that is very dear to you,' Mimir replied.

Odin thought hard. 'My eyes,' he said at last. 'I will sacrifice one of my eyes to drink from your spring.'

Mimir agreed. Odin put his mouth to the cool spring waters. When he had drunk long and deep, he looked around. Where were the runes, the symbols that contained all knowledge?

'You seek powerful magic, Odin,' Mimir's voice said. 'The runes come only to one who experiences death and lives again. Do you dare risk it?'

'I do.' Odin gazed up at Yggdrasil. Its windswept arms thrust against each other, inviting Odin up, challenging him. Odin began to climb. At the top of the tree, he wound his arms firmly around the branches. Now the wind could not dash him to the ground.

Fastened to the tree for nine days and nights, Odin was in agonies of thirst and starvation. He was so weak

Yggdrasil, also known as the World Tree, was an enormous ash tree whose branches covered the world. Its three main roots led underground to Mimir's spring, the Well of Urd, the home of the three Norns or goddesses who planned human fate and to Niflheim, the realm of the dead. The runes which appeared by the tree (see page 12) were the first alphabet and a few wise people were able to predict the future from the way they were arranged.

that his mind left his body and took him to places where he saw more with his one remaining eye than he had ever seen with two. He could hear secrets still inside the minds of those who thought them. He could move in an instant from one world to another.

'Living beings can't do this,' thought Odin. 'I must be dead. I've failed.'

The night that followed was long. Odin seemed to float above his body, watching it dangle, lifeless, in the branches of the tree. Then at last the rays of the rising sun made the world glitter. Now he would join the dead gods. But at least he would never again suffer the pain of the past nine days.

The next moment, a pain like a thunderbolt flashed through every part of Odin. He was back in his body! Far beneath him, by the foot of the tree, he could see strange strands of light flow into lines, triangles, knots.

'The runes!' Odin exclaimed. Swiftly he freed his arms and climbed down, gathering the glowing symbols to himself. Suddenly, he felt strong. It was the strength of someone who has known sacrifice, experienced death and in return acquired the greatest gift of all – the power of knowledge.

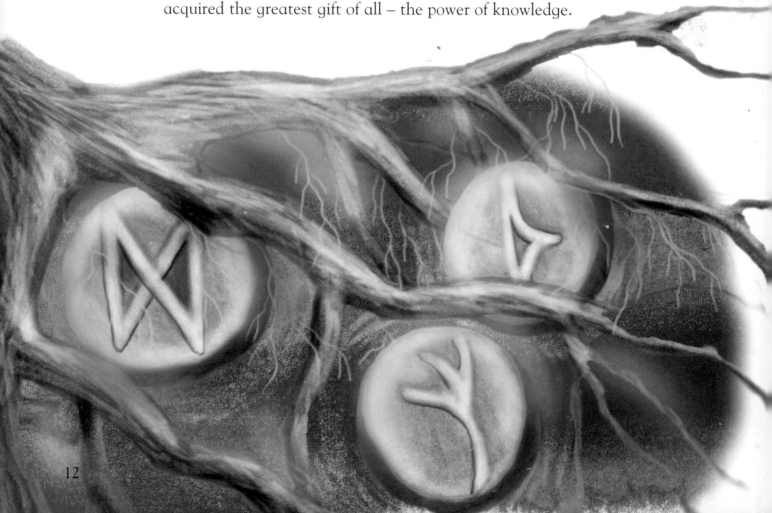

Viking Gods and Goddesses

The Aesir and the Vanir were the two groups of gods worshipped by the Vikings. When the Aesir first arrived in Scandinavia, they tried to take away the power of the Vanir. After fighting a war, they decided to live together. To ensure peace, they exchanged family members.

Ymir – the frost giant whose body formed the world

Vanir

Niord – god of the sea, fishing and treasure

Aesir

Bor – son of Buri, ancestor of the first gods

Frey – god of fertility, sunshine and rain

Freya – goddess of life, spring and growth, Frey's twin

Odin – ruler of the gods and god of mystery, magic and warriors. Wednesday is named after him

Frigg – goddess of humans, wife of Odin

Thor – god of the sky and a fierce warrior. Thursday is named after him

Heimdall – god of light and guardian of Bifrost, the rainbow bridge

Tyr – brave and wise god of war

Baldur – the shining god, son of Odin and Frigg

Hod – blind god of the night, Baldur's twin

Hermod – messenger to the gods

Loki – god of fire and trickster

Iormungand – the world serpent, son of Loki

Hel – ruler of the Underworld, daughter of Loki

Fenrir – fierce wolf, brother of Hel and Iormungand

Thor and the Giants

The early Vikings honoured the storm god Thor most of all because, like them, he was a warrior and made long journeys over harsh terrain. Thor fought for order against the giants who embodied chaos and that is why he was their greatest enemy. Thor's hammer, Miollnir, was the most powerful of all the gods' weapons. His worshippers used tiny models of it for luck.

Loki was the god of fire. He was a trickster god who helped the other gods but also got them into trouble to save himself. Loki had an evil side and the Vikings believed that he, along with his children, would destroy the world at Ragnarok (see page 21).

The Hammer of Thor

THOR OPENED HIS EYES, YAWNED AND REACHED FOR HIS TRUSTY HAMMER MIOLLNIR. It had vanished – stolen by the giants who were Thor's sworn enemies.

'The giants will destroy the gods and take over Asgard!' Thor bellowed to his friend Loki.

Loki nodded, troubled. 'Let's ask Freya for help.'

When Freya heard what had happened, she lent Loki her cloak of feathers. He soared high above the world, looking everywhere for the hammer. It was indeed in the land of the giants, which was also known as Iotunheim. A giant called Thrym had stolen it.

'Neither the gods of Aesir or Vanir can get it back,' bragged Thrym, 'unless Freya agrees to be my bride.'

Foolishly, Loki tried to persuade Freya to marry the giant. 'We'll rescue you as soon as Thrym gives back the hammer,' he assured her. But Freya was furious.

'How can you suggest such a thing?' she scolded him.

Loki narrowed his eyes. 'I have a better idea. Thor, you can pretend to be Freya!'

'I'm no woman!' thundered Thor, his great red beard bristling with the insult.

Even Freya had to laugh, imagining muscle-bound Thor in a bridal gown. 'Go on, Thor,' she giggled. 'It'll be worth it to get back Miollnir and save Asgard.'

Finally, Thor agreed. Freya dressed him in a fine veil and bridal gown and Loki escorted him to Iotunheim

where Thrym and his friends were enjoying the wedding feast.

'Here is Freya,' said Loki, seating the veiled Thor beside Thrym.

'What an enormous woman,' gasped Thrym.

'She is the great goddess of the Vanir,' Loki replied, trying not to smile. 'What did you expect? An elf?'

Thrym looked at his veiled bride wolfing down the wedding feast.

'She has a big appetite,' he remarked. 'And she's quite a drinker.'

'Ah!' sighed Loki, terrified that any moment now the game would be up. 'She's starved for love of you since the marriage was arranged.'

Flattered, Thrym gave the command Thor and Loki were waiting for.

'Bring the hammer to bless the bride!'

The hammer arrived and with a mighty roar, Thor seized it. The giants rose to attack him, but with Miollnir in his hand, Thor was invincible. The gods were safe again.

Thor and Iormungand

Thor was a fierce enemy of the World Serpent, Iormungand, who was the son of Loki and the giantess Angrboda. Iormungand coiled himself around the world, lurking in the mighty ocean which surrounded Yggdrasil. The Vikings believed that Thor and Iormungand would finally confront and destroy one another at Ragnarok.

ONCE A GIANT GAVE THOR SHELTER FOR THE NIGHT.

'Is it really you the Aesir boast about?' he mocked. 'You don't look fit to lift that old cat.'

Thor was insulted. He looked over at the limp creature and his cheeks blazed with fury. He grabbed the cat but it did not budge. Thor tried again. Still, it did not move. Soon, he was huffing and puffing.

'It's as heavy as a mountain,' he thought, giving it a final heave. The cat swung off the ground.

'Put it down, I beg you,' the giant pleaded.

Thor saw he was sweating with fear. 'What's the matter?' he asked, puzzled.

'That was no cat,' the giant confessed. 'It was Iormungand. Please let him go or the world will end.'

Thor reluctantly let go but he hadn't forgotten his rival. Soon he was able to challenge him again when he visited the home of a giant called Hymir.

'I'm going fishing,' Hymir announced rudely. 'You have to leave.'

'Why? I'll go fishing with you,' Thor replied.

Hymir laughed. 'You won't be able to stand the sea chill. You should stay on land.'

But Thor insisted, so Hymir told him to find some bait. Thor strode out and returned with a large ox's head. They both got into Hymir's boat and Thor started rowing vigorously.

'Stop,' Hymir said. 'The fishing is good here.'

Thor rowed on. 'We're getting close to Iormungand's territory,' Hymir warned.

Still Thor rowed on until they reached the centre of the ocean. With one throw, he flung out his line, baited with the ox-head. He felt a tug on his reel. Iormungand had taken the bait, but the fishing hook had lodged in his jaw and he thrashed about wildly, making Thor's hand smash against the side of the boat. Thor stamped down in pain. His feet went through the boat's bottom and hit the sea-bed. Instantly, Iormungand attacked, spitting venom in Thor's face. Thor reached for his hammer but before he could throw it, Hymir cut the reel and set Iormungand free. Once again, a giant had saved him from mighty Thor.

16

Geirrod and his daughters

In this story, Geirrod and his daughters Gialp and Greip represent the uncontrollable forces of nature such as floods, earthquakes and volcanic eruptions which the Vikings had to overcome, in order to survive. They saw Thor as their protector against the chaos of nature.

THE GIANT GEIRROD HAD INVITED THOR TO VISIT HIM IN IOTUNHEIM, BUT HE INSISTED THOR LEFT HIS INSTRUMENTS OF POWER BEHIND. 'He's up to something,' Thor thought, setting off to find out.

The journey was long and as night fell, Thor saw a hut and stopped to ask if he could spend the night there. A friendly giantess welcomed him in.

'Geirrod is a fierce fellow,' she said the next morning, learning of his purpose. 'Take these to help you.' She gave him a belt, a walking stick and some iron gloves. Thor thanked her and continued on his way.

Soon he came to the heaving river, Vimur. Thor put on his belt and started to wade across. Instantly, the waters rose until they reached his chin but the belt somehow kept him afloat. In the distance, stood Geirrod's daughter Gialp, grinning. Thor hurled a rock at her. Gialp fell back and Thor swam to safety across the river.

When he arrived at Geirrod's door he was sent to a shabby little hut. Thor slumped into the only chair in the room. This was no place for a guest and Thor would tell Geirrod so when he saw him. Suddenly, the chair wobbled under Thor and flew upwards. He felt his mighty body crushed against the ceiling. Thor thrust his stick hard against the rafters. Instantly, they smashed and the chair fell down with a crash. Gialp and her sister Greip fell to either side, shrieking and wailing. They had been under the chair!

Geirrod heard their screams. It was time to face Thor himself.

'You want a fight, Geirrod?' Thor roared, stepping into the giant's hall. 'Well, you'll get one.' As Thor raged, Geirrod hurled a brick of molten iron at him. Thor held up his hands, clad in the iron gloves. The brick flew back at Geirrod, crashing through a pillar, smashing the giant's skull and pushing him through a wall.

'That's what happens to giants who try to kill their guests!' Thor bellowed as he turned and strode furiously back to Asgard.

Tyr, the bravest God

Fenrir the wolf was one of the three children of Loki and Angrboda. When Odin was warned that Loki's children would destroy the world, he flung Iormungand into the sea and banished Hel to the Underworld. Here is how the gods dealt with Fenrir.

Fenrir snarled and snapped, straining against the chain with which the gods had bound him.

'He gets stronger every day,' laughed Loki, his father. But the other gods didn't join in. They had bound the fearsome wolf with countless strong chains, but every time he broke free. The Aesir decided to go to the dwarves. They were clever craftsmen and would know how to help.

'We will make a chain of six elements,' promised the dwarves. 'The lurking of a cat, the breath of a fish, the saliva of a bird, the muscles of a bear, the beard of a woman and the core of a mountain.'

When the chain was ready, the gods took it to Fenrir. 'Can you break this chain?' they asked.

Fenrir laughed at the flimsy cord. 'Are you trying to insult me?' he snarled. 'A worm could snap that piece of string.'

Then he narrowed his eyes. 'Unless it is some cunning magic? I want nothing to do with magic.'

'Poor Fenrir,' the gods mocked. 'Look how frightened he is of this frail chain.'

They mocked and teased until Fenrir agreed to be bound. But he had one condition. 'Throughout the contest, the hand of one god must remain in my mouth.'

The gods all fell silent. But Tyr, the mighty god of war, stepped forward and bravely put his hand in Fenrir's mouth. Swiftly, another god slipped the magic chain around the wolf's neck.

The contest began. Fenrir thrashed his neck from side to side, trying to break the chain. His jaws frothed and his coat grew dark with sweat. Tyr did not flinch.

At last, Fenrir realised he had been tricked. With a howl of fury, he clamped his teeth around Tyr's wrist, and bit off his hand.

Brave Tyr did not utter a word as the other gods rushed over to seize Fenrir. They slipped a sword between the wolf's teeth to stop him biting, then tethered him to a large rock.

'And there you shall stay until the world's end,' declared Odin.

The word Ragnarok means twilight or doom of the gods. According to the Voluspa, written around 1000 CE, at Ragnarok Fenrir will break his chains and his snarling jaws will open wide enough to reach from heaven to hell. Iormungand will raise a mighty tidal wave. A boat captained by Loki will carry the fire giant Surt of Muspell to a battle with the god Frey. Surt will defeat Frey and burn the world to a cinder.

Baldur, the Shining God

Most mythologies have a story in which a young god or goddess is trapped in the world of the dead. This was how ancient people explained summer and winter. Baldur, young and radiant, is like the sun in summer. His absence darkens the world and brings on winter. This story also tells us that the Vikings believed in life after death.

Odin's son, Baldur was having nightmares. Odin was very worried about him. He decided to visit an oracle who could tell him Baldur's future.

'Hel's people await Baldur,' the oracle told Odin.

Greatly saddened, Odin returned to his wife Frigg and told her of the oracle's words.

'But everyone loves Baldur,' said Frigg. 'Who would want to kill him?'

Odin shook his head. 'She would not say.'

Frigg travelled the earth, asking all living things to promise they would not harm Baldur. The air, the plants, the mountains and waters, all gave her their word. Baldur would never die – neither poison nor metal nor disease would harm him. To prove it, the gods invented a game. They hurled all kinds of things at Baldur but nothing could hurt him.

Loki was jealous of the young, handsome god. 'Baldur is more popular than ever,' he grumbled. 'I have to put an end to it.' Loki disguised himself as an old woman and visited Frigg.

'Is it true that every animal, mineral and vegetable made this promise?' he asked.

'All but a tiny mistletoe near Valhalla. It was too young to understand,' Frigg whispered.

Loki could hardly contain his glee. He flew to Valhalla, ripped out the mistletoe and returned to Asgard where the gods were playing their favourite game. A little apart from the rest stood Hod, Baldur's twin.

'Why aren't you joining in?' Loki asked.

'You know quite well I'm blind,' Hod said.

'Be a sport for once,' Loki said. He thrust the mistletoe into Hod's hand and directed his throw. The mistletoe pierced Baldur and he fell to the ground, dead. As the gods and goddesses mourned, Loki fled.

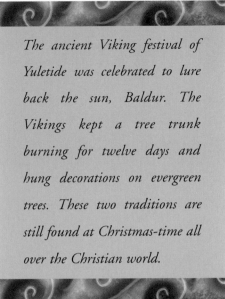

The ancient Viking festival of Yuletide was celebrated to lure back the sun, Baldur. The Vikings kept a tree trunk burning for twelve days and hung decorations on evergreen trees. These two traditions are still found at Christmas-time all over the Christian world.

The gods placed Baldur on his longboat along with many treasures. As the boat burst into flames, the god Hermod leapt on Sleipner's back and crossed Gioll, the long river to the Underworld.

'Set Baldur free,' he told the goddess Hel. 'All living things weep for him.'

'Then let their tears wash him out of the Underworld,' she replied scornfully.

Hermod immediately sent out Hel's message. Every living creature wept for Baldur, except a giantess called Thokki, who jeered: 'Let Hel keep him.'

And so Baldur remained in the Land of the Dead. But the gods suspected that Thokki was Loki in disguise. They tied him to three rocks where he will stay until the end of the world.

Sigurd's Quest

This story is from Volsungsaga, a 13th century Scandinavian saga telling of King Volsung of Hunland and his son Sigmund, a famous hero of Viking mythology. A saga is a tale spanning many generations. The third part of Volsungsaga follows the adventures of Sigmund's son, Sigurd, another Viking hero.

PRINCE SIGURD WAS HAPPY LIVING IN THE KINGDOM OF DENMARK UNDER THE PROTECTION OF THE KING. The court swordsmith, Regin, was busy teaching him all that a young prince needed to know of fighting and travelling and wisdom and Sigurd was an eager pupil.

One day Regin told Sigurd about a great hoard of treasure that lay in a cave guarded by the monster Fafnir. 'You should kill him and seize the treasure,' Regin urged.

Sigurd agreed, full of enthusiasm. Regin prepared a sword for his quest. But when Sigurd practised using his new sword, its blade fell apart. Regin made another sword, and this time too the blade shattered.

Sigurd remembered his mother had saved the pieces of his father's sword which was said to be unconquerable. He gave them to Regin, who melted them down and crafted a sword strong enough to slice through metal and sharp enough to cut through string in a flowing river.

Sigurd was impatient to begin his adventure. 'Can I borrow a horse to go on a quest?' he asked the king.

'Choose one from my stable,' the king replied.

Sigurd eyed the horses in awe. They were all magnificent. How could he choose?

'What about this one?' a voice suggested. Sigurd turned to see a hooded stranger. It was Odin in disguise. He pointed to a lively stallion, Grani, the son of his own horse Sleipnir. Sigurd wasted no time. He mounted Grani and rode off with Regin. At last they arrived at a cave hidden deep in the mountains.

Regin pointed to the ground. 'See those footprints? Fafnir has gone to have a drink. Dig a trench on this path. When Fafnir returns, strike at his belly from below and kill him.'

As Sigurd was digging, the hooded stranger appeared again. 'The monster's blood is poisonous,' he warned. 'Dig some pits beside your trench. Then the blood will flow away without harming you.'

'Strange,' thought Sigurd, 'Regin never warned me about Fafnir's blood.' Again, he did as Odin advised and jumped out of the way as soon as he had struck the monster. Regin reappeared as Fafnir's blood drained into the pits. He put his hand to the monster's wound and pulled out its heart while Sigurd looked on in disgust. 'Roast this,' Regin commanded. 'I will return later to eat it.' Sigurd built a fire and skewered the monster's heart to the spit.

The heart sizzled and frothed as it cooked over the flames and its hot juice spattered on to Sigurd's thumb. Sigurd sucked hard at it to stop the searing pain. Suddenly, he realised that he could understand the language of the birds. They were talking about him!

'Poor Sigurd doesn't realise that Regin's really a monster,' twittered one bird.

'Do you think he'll kill Sigurd once he's got his hands on the gold?' asked his companion.

'Why not?' replied the first bird. 'He killed his father for it – and his brother.'

The birds discussed how the god Loki, out hunting, had accidentally shot Regin's brother, Otter. Regin's father had demanded a ransom of gold from Loki which the god had cunningly tricked out of a dwarf. Regin killed his father for the gold, but then found that his other brother, Fafnir, had taken it.

'Sigurd should kill him first and take the gold. Then he can ride to the Hinderfiall Mountains to rescue the brave warrior that no one else can save,' decided the bird.

Sigurd could not believe his ears. Regin had pretended to be his friend so that he could kill him and take the gold. Now Sigurd was forced to kill or be killed, so he chopped off Regin's head, seized the gold and rode off in search of the Hinderfiall Mountains.

As he neared the mountains, he saw a bright flickering light before him, leaping and dancing.

'Come on my friend,' he said to Grani, 'let's jump through it.' With a mighty bound Grani brought Sigurd through the fire and into a courtyard held up by stone pillars. In its centre lay a fully armed warrior.

Sigurd walked slowly up to the still figure, every bit

of it covered in armour. Who could it be?

Sigurd pulled his sword Gram from his belt and ran its point round the helmet. The armour fell away, revealing a beautiful young woman dressed in white.

The woman sat up. 'My name is Brynhild,' she told Sigurd. 'I am a Valkyrie. I help heroes in battle.'

Brynhild explained that Odin had told her to help a warrior called Helmut Gunnar win a battle. But between battles, she had turned herself into a swan and, as she swam, one of Helmut's enemies had stolen her clothes. 'He refused to return them unless I helped him. So Helmut lost the battle and Odin punished my disobedience by putting me to sleep here in a ring of fire. He said that unless a hero came who was brave enough to leap through the fire, I would lie here forever.'

Sigurd was delighted he had saved Brynhild. From that day on, many called him the 'Fire-walker'.

Glossary

Aesir – one of the two families of gods worshipped by the Vikings. The other family was called the Vanir. The Aesir appeared in Scandinavia after the Vanir, but after an almighty battle, described in many ancient Viking myths, the two families of gods decided to live together in peace.

Asgard – the land of the Viking gods, also known as Godland.

Baldur – the shining god who was the son of Odin and Frigg. He was killed by the jealous god Loki and sent to live in Hel, the Land of the Dead.

Bifrost – the rainbow bridge which linked Asgard to Midgard. It was guarded by the watchman god, Heimdall.

Draupnir – a magical gold ring belonging to Odin, which was made by the dwarves. It was extremely valuable, for every nine days it created eight new gold rings.

Ginnungagap – the great void or empty space which separated the lands of Niflheim and Muspell before the world was created.

Hel – the Land of the Dead, where people went when they had died of sickness or old age. It was ruled over by the hideous goddess Hel, daughter of the god Loki.

ice age – a period of time in the Earth's history when a large part of its surface was covered in ice. The last major ice age happened around 20,000 years ago.

Iotunheim – the land of the giants, also known as Giantland.

Loki – the god of fire and magic. Although he was a friend of the Aesir gods, he often caused trouble for them. The Vikings believed that he, along with his three evil children Iormungand, Hel and Fenrir, would help to bring about the end of the world at Ragnarok.

longboat – a Viking ship with a square sail and many oars. At traditional Viking funerals, the body of the dead person was placed on a longboat which was set alight and sent out to sea. The boats were often heaped with treasures which would help the person on their journey to the Land of the Dead.

Midgard – the land created by Odin and his brothers, where humankind lived. It was also known as Middle Earth.

Mimir's spring – the sacred spring which was believed to be the source of all knowledge. It was guarded by the giant Mimir and found beneath the roots of Yggdrasil, the World Tree.

Miollnir – Thor's mighty hammer which always hit its target and returned safely to Thor afterwards. It was made for Thor by the dwarves and had magic powers.

Muspell – the land of fire which was found to the south of Ginnungagap. It was ruled by Surt.

mythology – the collection or study of myths.

Niflheim – the dark, frozen land which was found north of Ginnungagap. It was also known as the land of the dead, or Hel.

Odin – the father of the Viking gods. In some countries he was known as Woden, which is how Wednesday came to be named after him.

oracle – a priest or priestess through whom the gods were believed to speak. People consulted them to ask questions about the future, and the answers could come in the voice of a god or in a dream.

Ragnarok – the Viking name for the end of the world. The Vikings believed that this would come about in a mighty battle between good and bad, in which the gods would fight against the evil forces of Loki and his three children. In the end, Asgard would be destroyed by fire and many gods would die. Following this, a new, better world would be created. Ragnarok also means 'twilight of the gods.'

runes – these ancient symbols made up letters in an early alphabet. The runes represented knowledge to the Vikings. In Viking mythology, they appeared among the roots of Yggdrasil to those who, like Odin, had gained very great wisdom.

Scandinavia – a name for some of the countries of northern Europe, including Norway, Sweden and Denmark.

Sleipnir – a magical eight-legged horse which could run and fly faster than the wind. It belonged to the god Odin.

Thor – the mighty god of thunder and storms. The Vikings worshipped him for his strength and courage in battle.

Valhalla – a great hall where warriors killed in battle were ruled over by Odin. At Ragnarok, they would come back to life and fight with the gods against evil.

Valkyries – beautiful warrior-maidens who served Odin. They carried the bodies of heroes killed in battle to Valhalla.

Vanir – the older family of Viking gods.

Vikings – a race of Scandinavians who lived from approximately 800-1100 CE. They are famous for having been fierce sea-faring warriors who conquered and settled large areas of Europe during their rule.

Well of Urd – a spring found beneath the roots of Yggdrasil. According to Viking mythology, three goddesses called Norns lived beside the well. They decided people's fates.

Yggdrasil – a giant ash tree which was found at the centre of the earth. Its enormous branches covered the world, while its three main roots led below ground to Mimir's spring, the Well of Urd and Niflheim, the realm of the dead. Yggdrasil was also called the World Tree.

Ymir – the frost giant who was formed where Niflheim and Muspell met when the world was created. He was killed by Odin and his brothers, who believed he made the world too cold to live in. They put his body in Ginnungagap and used it to create the land of Midgard.

Index